Original title:
The Ocean's Soft Voice

Copyright © 2025 Creative Arts Management OÜ
All rights reserved.

Author: Ethan Prescott
ISBN HARDBACK: 978-1-80587-454-6
ISBN PAPERBACK: 978-1-80587-924-4

Songs of Rock and Tidal Pool

The crab in his shell, thinks he's quite the star,
Snap, snap, snap, he's a rock and roll guitar.
Starfish is a dancer, legs in a twirl,
While the seaweed giggles, in a slick green whirl.

The fish have a party, with bubbles galore,
Shaking their fins on the ocean floor.
Clams are the bouncers, with pearls in their grip,
"Uh-oh!" yells a shrimp, "I'm about to flip!"

Echoing Along the Shore

Seagulls are gossiping, flapping away,
"Did you see the sandsuit that crab wore today?"
The tides chuckle softly, as they lap at the land,
While kids build their castles, a moisture-filled band.

A dolphin rolls over, with a wink and a leap,
"Join my conga line, let's make a big heap!"
Shells clap their hands, in a rhythmic delight,
As the starfish sing songs, through the day and the night.

Melodies from the Abyss

In the deep, deep blue, where shadows seem shy,
A fish with a top hat is passing by.
He tips it and bows, with elegance rare,
While a squid in the back tries to style his own hair.

From sea cucumbers, you hear a faint tune,
"Dance with me, darling, under the blue moon!"
An octopus juggles as bubbles float free,
"Who thought nightlife was this wild at sea?"

Chants of the Seafoam Knights

The seafrogs croak songs, loud and absurd,
With bubbles as melodies, strange as their word.
The whales join the chorus, with harmonies grand,
While the villainous sardines form a sneaky band.

With sea foam as armor, they march on the sand,
"Fear not, for we're here, the role is quite planned!"
The sea urchins cheer with spikes held up high,
"Save the day, noble knights, give it a try!"

Songs of Solitude at Sea

Sailing on a purple blob,
Seagulls squawking like my mob,
Fish are chatting, quite a lot,
Judging me, but I'm still hot.

A crab waves with its little claw,
Cracking jokes that leave me in awe,
Mermaids giggle just out of sight,
Splashing waves hide their delight.

I brought a sandwich, but it flew,
Dolphin said, 'Guess it's for me too!'
Saltwater tickles my toes so bright,
Who knew the sea had such a bite?

These waves laugh like they know my name,
Teasing me in this silly game,
With every splash, a new surprise,
The sea's a joker in disguise.

Murmurs in the Coral Garden

Underwater whispers all around,
Clownfish giggle without a sound,
Coral reefs seem to conspire,
To prank the fish with bubbles dire.

An octopus plays hide-and-seek,
Inking jokes every time we peek,
Sea turtles dance, they've got some flair,
While starfish just sit, but who'd dare?

A pufferfish blows up with pride,
Sprouting jokes from inside, quite wide,
While shrimp steal snacks, oh what a sight,
In this garden, it's pure delight.

The jellyfish sway like disco balls,
Drifting through watery, glitzy halls,
Their transparent giggles warmly glow,
Quite the party in the ocean's flow.

The Serenade of Sunset Waves

As the sun dips, the waves applaud,
Flipping fish show off, how odd!
Seagulls swoop, with perfect flair,
As sunset paints the sky with care.

A crab struts by, in a little hat,
Singing tunes, imagine that!
Dancing shadows on the sand,
All these antics, oh so grand.

Whales hum low, a bassy beat,
Joining in on this rhythmic feat,
The tide rolls in with a goofy sway,
Who knew twilight could be this play?

With laughter echoing on the breeze,
Every creature aiming to please,
As night wraps up this caper so bright,
The ocean's cheer drifts into night.

Lull into the Water's Embrace

Float along on a fluffy tide,
Where the sea's ticklish sides abide,
Barnacles crack dad jokes all day,
While sleepy waves just toss and sway.

Mermaids nap with a flip and a flop,
Singing lullabies that never stop,
A wave winks, with a cheeky grin,
As fishes shuffle, letting dreams begin.

Bubbles pop like giggles in the air,
While seaweed sways without a care,
The sun's warm hug makes all things fine,
As I chuckle at this world divine.

Here in the deep, where dreams collide,
With every splash, my worries slide,
Embraced by whimsy beneath the stars,
The water rocks me—no need for bars.

Tranquil Waters' Embrace

Waves giggle and splash all around,
They whisper secrets, not making a sound.
Fish in tuxedos dance in a line,
Jelly's just jiggling, feeling just fine.

A crab reads a book, with glasses askew,
While seagulls debate who's the best at a cue.
Shells sing along, making quite a racket,
And dolphins bring snacks, defying the packet.

The Sea's Gentle Patter

A sea turtle winks, then takes a slow dive,
With a splashy laugh, he's happy and jive.
Starfish clap hands, on a dance floor of sand,
They've got the moves, oh isn't it grand?

Seashells in chorus, sing tales from afar,
While octopuses juggle, they're quite the bazaar.
The tide joins the fun, with a bubbly cheer,
It's a party down here, let's all interfere!

Melodies of the Shimmering Blue

Goldfish are gossiping, spreading the news,
While seaweeds twirl in their glittery shoes.
A narwhal's got style, with his pointy, cool hat,
He's got a sharp look and a charming chit-chat.

Corals are trading their best fashion tips,
And swordfish are fencing, with elegant flips.
The sea sings a tune, with bubbles that pop,
As everyone laughs, they just won't stop!

Chords of the Nautical Realm

Crabs in their meetings share jokes from the tide,
While dolphins make jokes that they cannot abide.
The sea cucumbers hum in delight,
While sea urchins grin, feeling quite light.

With driftwood guitars, they strum a wild beat,
Anemones sway, tapping their feet.
A narwhal solo, oh what a surprise,
As the waves join the fun, under blue, sunny skies.

Sonnet of Storms and Serenity

Waves dance high, a playful sight,
Seagulls squawk with all their might.
Shells are tossed like frisky toys,
While dolphins leap with joyful noise.

Rain comes down, a splashy mess,
Umbrellas flip, oh what a stress.
Splash a clown in wet disguise,
As laughter echoes in the skies.

But calm returns, a gentle tease,
A breeze that whispers through the trees.
Kids build castles, grand and tall,
While ocean waves just giggle, enthrall.

So here we are, with grit and glee,
Enjoying all, from land to sea.
Every drop and every wave,
Brings a grin we gladly crave.

Tapestry of the Wind-Kissed Sea

Sandy toes and sunscreen red,
A seagull's quest for crumbs instead.
Beach balls bounce, a joyful sight,
While kids throw sand, oh what a fright!

A crab scuttles, all in haste,
Waving claws, it's quite the taste!
Giggles rise with each wipeout,
Surfboards tumble, splash about.

Kites soar high, they dance and twist,
An octopus who looks quite p—d.
With every wave, a happy chant,
As starfish wiggle and seaweed plants.

So let's dive in, and ride the tide,
With laughter strong, we cannot hide.
In this tapestry, bright and free,
The joy we find is a sight to see.

Voices in the Swell

Chubby seals in sunlit grace,
Barking loud, they win the race.
Surfboards wobble, balance is key,
As laughter rises, wild and free.

Seashells whisper secrets bold,
While jellyfish just float and scold.
A skip and hop, a splash and play,
In their silly, wobbly ballet.

Crabs in suits, all lined for show,
Tap dance odd, with a crabby glow.
Fish swim by with curious eyes,
While seagulls plot their next surprise.

In this wild, wavy parade,
Joy and chaos cleverly made.
With every splash, a giggle sounds,
The voices echo 'round the grounds.

Serene Currents

Bubbles rise in gentle rolls,
As fishies giggle with tiny shoals.
Mermaids come to share a laugh,
While dolphins show off their autograph.

Sandy castles melt away,
As tides tease more than kids can play.
A beach ball flies, a misplaced aim,
And splashes turn to laughter's fame.

Paddleboards wobble, surfers cheer,
The sea's a friend, never a fear.
But a wave's surprise, oh what a splash,
Turns laughter into a sudden crash.

So let's embrace this wavy jest,
Where waves and giggles are truly best.
In every flick and twirl we find,
Life's a jest, both sweet and kind.

Lullaby of the Sea

Waves tickle toes as they dance,
Seagulls squawk in a cheeky prance.
Starfish gossip with shells nearby,
Crabs throw shade as they scuttle by.

The sun slips down, a golden flair,
Fish flip-flop with a splash and glare.
Sandcastles smile, proud and tall,
But watch for tides, they'll take the fall.

Picnics laugh with a sandwich roar,
Seashells hum, a sandy score.
With each swoosh and swoon of tide,
Good vibes abound, and worries slide.

Underneath, the mermaids tease,
Doing flips with utmost ease.
They wink as they swim, quite the show,
While we just float and go with flow.

Murmurs of the Blue

Whales make jokes in ocean's depth,
Kraken shares its secret prep.
The fish wear hats, a sight to see,
As dolphins giggle while sipping tea.

The tide leaves snacks upon the shore,
Shells hold secrets of legend lore.
But careful now, don't lose a shoe,
The waves might steal just out of view.

Octopi have a fashion spree,
Tentacles twirl with utmost glee.
They'll dress you up in seaweed flair,
While laughing fishes float in air.

A crab walks by with a royal strut,
While puffers puff, not one to cut.
"Life's a beach!" they chant with cheer,
While sandcastles grow without a fear.

Secrets of the Distant Horizon

The horizon wears a silly grin,
While pirates dance and share their gin.
Mermaids surf on waves of fun,
Chasing crabs under the sun.

Seashells giggle, they tell tall tales,
Of fish who sail with paper sails.
A treasure map drawn in the sand,
Leads to chocolate, oh so grand!

Surfers wipe out, but take a bow,
For every splash is just a wow.
Ocean foam fights with a sandy foot,
While sea cucumbers strut like soot.

The sun dips low, casting a beam,
As fish practice their nightly dream.
With laughter loud, the waves retreat,
In this silly world, we feel complete.

Caress of the Brine

Waves whisper jokes upon the shore,
As crabs break out in dance and roar.
The water flicks with a cheeky hand,
Tickling toes in the soft, warm sand.

Salty breezes carry a song,
Where the dolphin troupe swings along.
They flip and dive with a splash so neat,
Inviting us all to join their beat.

Seagull swoops, a thief in sight,
Stealing chips with all its might.
The beach ball bounces, 'round we go,
Dodging waves in a playful show.

At twilight's glow, the stories spin,
Of fish who wear a silly grin.
With laughter shared, we twirl and twine,
In the warm embrace of the brine.

Luminous Tide's Embrace

Bubbles dance with glee and cheer,
As fish wear hats and crack a beer.
Seagulls squawk their silly songs,
While crabs perform their silly prongs.

Waves laugh softly, tickle toes,
Shells join in with silly prose.
A starfish juggles with great flair,
While dolphins plot to steal our hair.

Turtles wear their shades so bright,
Surfboards flipping in pure delight.
The beach ball rolls, no one knows how,
A game of chase, we're lost in wow!

In this realm of watery fun,
We'll dance 'til day is nearly done.
With friends so quirky, life's a spree,
In tides that swell with joy and glee.

Whispers Under the Celestial Dome

Under stars, the waves confess,
Octopuses in a party dress.
Fish gossip as they swim around,
While jellyfish dance without a sound.

The moon's a mime, it pulls the tide,
And all our worries take a ride.
Seaweed giggles, swaying slow,
The night is young, let laughter flow.

Crabs hold court, their rule is fair,
With sandy thrones, they take the air.
Their royal decrees? A dance-off game,
To see who gets the funniest name!

So join the fun beneath the night,
Where every wave brings pure delight.
In salty air, let humor swim,
As laughter echoes on a whim.

The Calm Before the Surf

In the calm, the seagulls plot,
A beach ball war? Oh, why not?
With timidity, the crabs unite,
To throw a party, oh what a sight!

Before the chaos of the waves,
They dance like dancers from the caves.
Clams giggle, sharing their lore,
While sea stars laugh from the ocean floor.

Sandy feet and sunscreen flies,
With each splash, a big surprise.
The dolphins tease and flip with grace,
Making everyone laugh in this place.

So here's to the calm, short-lived fun,
Before the splash, before we run.
In every quiet, giggle blooms,
Let joy erupt before it zooms!

Ballad of the Twilight Waters

As twilight settles, seashells hum,
Crabs breakdance, oh look, here they come!
The tide rolls in like a playful pup,
With waves that giggle and never give up.

Eels tell jokes that slither and sway,
While starfish teach us how to play.
A sandcastle king waves with delight,
While the tide sneaks in, ready to bite.

Waves crash softly in a funny spree,
Paddling through what's left of tea.
A porpoise wears a goofy grin,
Chasing bubbles, he jumps right in.

So gather near as night unfolds,
With whispers of laughter, stories told.
In twilight's glow, joy takes flight,
As waters shimmer with pure delight.

Ballads of Old Sailors' Spirits

There once was a sailor named Fred,
Who lost his best hat in a spread.
He sang to the breeze,
And begged on his knees,
"Come back, or I'll drown in my dread!"

The gulls laughed and danced overhead,
As he chased after fish near the bed.
He slipped on a shell,
With a sudden loud yell,
And wondered why he ever fled.

His mates, they all found it quite grand,
To see Fred flailing in the sand.
They called him a clown,
As they mopped him down,
And wished he would stick to the plan.

But Fred, full of laughter and glee,
Declared, "I'll face waves like a spree!"
He twirled like a whiz,
Forgetting the fizz,
And danced with a crab by a tree.

The Language of Salty Spray

A dolphin with dreams on a spree,
Wore glasses, thought he was a bee.
He buzzed through the waves,
With all his sea braves,
And puzzled the fish with his glee.

A crab claimed he was quite the chef,
And cooked all the fish to their death.
Yet every fish found,
When they looked around,
He's really just baking his meth!

A starfish who prided his flair,
Wore polish and boasted his share.
"I'm classy and chic,
Not just some old freak!"
His friends could only give a stare.

And so in this world of the brine,
The humor of sea life does shine.
With laughter and fun,
They danced 'til they spun,
In the deep where the bubbles entwine.

Whispers Beneath the Waves

A clam had a secret to tell,
He whispered it close to a shell.
The fish rolled their eyes,
In colorful sighs,
"Why's clams always shushing so well?"

The octopus, sly in his ways,
Played tricks on fish most of the days.
With eight arms on deck,
He'd spin them a wreck,
While they swam in their filtered malaise.

One day in the bright coral reef,
A sea turtle floated in grief.
"I swim like a rock,
I'm really no jock,"—
Yet he loved to pretend he was chief.

But laughter arose from the sand,
As the creatures in harmony planned.
For beneath every laugh,
Was joy in the craft,
Of living in this wavy land.

The Calm Before the Storm

The sea was as smooth as a gin,
Not a fish dared to wiggle or spin.
They shared tales galore,
Of storms that once swore,
"We'll never let lightning in!"

A crab with a penchant for tales,
Said, "Listen, my friends, to my wails.
The last storm was mad,
It drove all us bad,
To dance with the winds and the gales!"

A mackerel piped up with a grin,
"Oh, I'm not afraid of the din!
I'll jump back and forth,
From the south to the north,
As long as I find a good fin!"

And so they made merry with jest,
In a lull that felt truly blessed.
Before thunder would pound,
They laughed all around,
With a wave that just wouldn't let rest.

The Allure of the Ocean's Breath

Waves crash loud, then hush so sweet,
A sea of giggles, tickling feet.
Fish in tuxedos swim with flair,
They wink at seagulls just to stare.

Shells stacked high like tiny hats,
The crabs engage in funny chats.
They dance a jig, oh what a sight,
While dolphins join, the mood's just right.

Tides whisper tales of boats that sink,
Like socks that vanish, oh what a stink!
With every splash, laughter ensues,
As salty breezes spread the news.

Mermaids giggle, tugging at nets,
Boys grabbing snacks—blame it on pets!
With every wave comes a riddle or two,
As seaweed twirls in the ocean's brew.

The Lure of Salted Dreams

In the morning, the tide pulls back,
Leaving treasures on sand's bright track.
Crabs play hide and seek, oh so sly,
As gulls steal fries, not even shy.

Starfish compete in yoga poses,
While jellyfish dance in bright pink roses.
The sandcastles topple, yet they don't fret,
For tides will come to clear all regret.

Sandy toes and giggles galore,
Seashells tell jokes, leaving us wanting more.
With every splash, we burst into laughter,
Wishing this warmth would go on ever after.

Beach balls bounce, like dreams on the shore,
While sunburns happen— who could ask for more?
The lure of this place is quite hard to beat,
Especially with ice cream dripping sweet.

Whispered Promises of the Sea

The gulls are squawking, what a loud choir,
As they plot to steal fries, it seems desired.
Waves roll in, tickling our toes,
While fish tease with their wiggly shows.

Seashells gossip, oh what do they know?
Of sailors' tales and currents aglow.
With a squint of the eye, a prankster appears,
As seaweed threads its way through our fears.

Sandcastles rise like dreams in the sun,
But here comes the tide, oh what's to be done?
Laughter erupts as towers descend,
Making beach play a whimsical trend.

A crab in sunglasses strolls with such pride,
While the sea whispers secrets on the tide.
With every ripple, a chuckle we share,
In this watery place, nothing can compare.

Shadows of Stormy Serenades

Clouds march in like an army, so grey,
But we dance on the beach, come what may.
Storms may threaten, wind in our hair,
Yet we jump in puddles without a care.

Waves crash high, making a ruckus,
While fish play tag, acting all gutsy.
Seagulls squawk out jokes from above,
As lightning tickles, falls in love.

Rainy socks squish, a slippery war,
As laughter erupts, it's never a bore.
With every flash of lightning's delight,
We sing crazy songs in the dimming light.

The shadows dance in the fading sun,
Reminding us all that storms are just fun.
In the heart of chaos, find joy, don't delay,
For after the rain, sunshine holds sway.

Lament of the Lighthouse Keeper

A beacon shines for ships in need,
Yet seagulls squawk, while I take heed.
They tease my hats and steal my lunch,
A lighthouse life proves quite the hunch.

I dream of days with cozy chats,
Not dodging birds or sneaky bats.
Yet here I stand, tall and bright,
With salty breeze as my delight.

The waves might crash, the fog may roll,
But it's the birds that take their toll.
I shout at them, "You pesky crew!"
But all they do is steal my stew!

Next time I'll bring an extra snack,
To fend off all their endless flack.
A lighthouse keeper's plight is real,
But I just laugh, it's quite the deal.

Sounds of the Surfing Path

A surfer's grin, a splash, a cheer,
Yet one wrong turn—oh, what a fear!
He wipes out hard, the waves will jest,
As all his friends say, "Nice try, best!"

The ocean winks with frothy fun,
"A twist, a turn, oh look, he's done!"
With surfboards flying all around,
Who knew that waves could be so sound?

The splash of water, everyone's shout,
A sea of laughter, no room for doubt.
But wipeouts happen, it's a blast,
As folks recount their glories past.

Yet still they ride, the fearless crew,
Embracing each wave, like tornadoes blue.
With laughter echoing on the shore,
The tales they'll tell, we all adore.

The Embrace of Vapors and Vessels

A ship sails in, looking quite spry,
But who knew it'd kiss a cloud so high?
With vapors dancing, the sailors shout,
"I knew we'd end up in a pout!"

The fog rolls in like a cuddly cat,
Hiding treasures, and also a brat.
"Where's the land?" the captain cries,
While seagulls giggle, the poor guy sighs.

With cannons blasting and dreams of gold,
Turns out the map was just too bold.
The compass spins, the crew's a mess,
They laugh and sing through all the stress.

In fog, they float like ships in space,
In silly hats and frantic grace.
Yet when they find the shore again,
A tale of laughs must now begin.

Forgotten Chants of the Brine

The fish do sing, or so they claim,
But it sounds more like a goofy game.
With bubbles popping, a tune so rare,
Who knew the sea had such flair?

The crabs get groovy in their own way,
Dancing to beats of a kelp bouquet.
"Clap your claws!" a clam will cheer,
Yet most just roll their eyes in fear.

The jellyfish float, looking so grand,
As they wave their tentacles, oh, so bland.
"Is that a song or just a jest?"
The fish reply, "We're doing our best!"

But when the tide turns, their show is done,
They go back home, their day's been fun.
In silence now, they grumble and pout,
While humans laugh, "What's that about?"

Traces of Lapping Waters

The waves play tag, a playful dance,
They splash and giggle, a sea-born trance.
A crab with glasses, winks at the sun,
While seagulls laugh, oh what fun!

A dolphin dives, with a silly twist,
Wearing seaweed like a fancy wrist.
Starfish clap as they cheer so loud,
For the fish parade that makes them proud.

The tide rolls in, with a cheeky grin,
Whispers of salt, where laughter begins.
Jellyfish join with a wobbly wave,
In this sea of chuckles, we're all brave.

Smiling seashells share their best jokes,
While clownfish dance, with funny pokes.
The sun sets low, in colors so bright,
But this ocean fun won't end tonight!

Notes of the Gentle Surf

Whispers on the shore, like a ticklish breeze,
The waves crack up, as they tease the trees.
A surfer slips, does an epic faceplant,
While sandcastles giggle, as if they can chant.

Kelp takes a bow, adds flair to the scene,
With a wink from a crab, who's feeling quite keen.
Pelicans dive, but miss by a mile,
As children point, and laugh with a smile.

Seashells gossip, and share their best tales,
Of fish with mustaches, and laughing whales.
The tide tips over, with a bubbly cheer,
Playing the tune that all fish hold dear.

Oh, the sea rolls on, with a pun or two,
Inviting all creatures to join in the cue.
With splashes and giggles, the night is alive,
In this water world, the laughter will thrive!

Oceanic Reveries

Bubbles rise like laughter, up to the sky,
Fishes tell secrets, as the currents sigh.
A starfish yawns, takes a nap on a rock,
While octopuses dance, around the clock.

A wave whispers jokes, in a ticklish tone,
As sea cucumbers pretend they're on loan.
With sea turtles racing, half the time slow,
And clams sharing gossip that only they know.

Splashing around, the corals will grin,
For every little wave is a cheerful spin.
The tide plays a tune that tickles the heart,
Where every laugh and splash is a fine work of art.

So come join the fun, let's frolic and play,
In this watery haven where joy finds its way.
With a wink and a wave, let's embrace the light,
As the ocean chuckles, it feels so right!

The Sea's Whispering Heart

The shore hums a tune, oh what a jest,
With waves that giggle, they never rest.
A fish with a bowtie swims by with a wink,
As crabs share secrets over a curious drink.

A sandpiper skips, with a hop and a prance,
While clams have a raucous, undersea dance.
The tide rolls in with a playful shout,
Shaking the sand, it's a laugh-out-loud bout.

Whirling and twirling, the seaweed sways,
With jellyfish jiving in spontaneous ways.
A sea urchin frowns, but soon can't resist,
As lobsters join in for a comedic twist.

With humor afloat, and silliness near,
The ocean invites us to join in the cheer.
So let's splash around, with giggles we'll part,
For the laughter of waters, is a gift from the heart!

Whispers of the Deep

In the sea, a fish with a tie,
Gives speeches to crabs, oh my!
They chuckle and roll, full of glee,
While turtles just sip their green tea.

A jellyfish floats with a grin,
Waving hello, waving like kin.
With a bounce in its step, it's a sight,
Dancing like disco, under moonlight.

A seaweed band plays a tune,
While seagulls pop in, to swoon.
With rhythm and rhyme, they all prance,
Making the waves join the dance.

So if you stop by, take a listen,
The sea has jokes that are glisten.
With laughs and splashes, they all share,
The ocean's humor fills the air.

Serenade of the Waves

The splashy waves sing their song,
To dolphins who dance all day long.
A clam bursts out, saying, 'Hey!'
Jumping in rhythm, come what may!

A crab in a hat, very chic,
With pinchers that tap, oh so sleek.
He tells a joke, then takes a bow,
Making all the starfish go 'Wow!'

The sea foam swirls, it's a sight,
Tickling toes, oh what a delight!
And fishy friends swim in a line,
With a giggle that's just divine.

Under the sun, they frolic and play,
In a waterslide made of ray.
The sea's silly whispers never cease,
A world of laughter, joy, and peace.

Echoes Beneath the Surface

Bubbles rise with a giggle and pop,
As octopus makes a funny flop.
With every swirl, there's a playful jest,
A splash of humor that never rests.

In the depths, where the sea things dwell,
A fish tells tales of how he fell.
With every wiggle, the laughter spreads,
While snails in the corner shake their heads.

A sea cucumber tells a pun,
While lounging around, having fun.
"Why did the starfish cross the bay?
To get to the other tide, hooray!"

The whispers echo, soft and bright,
In a game of tag beneath starlight.
With a touch of whimsy, they all play,
In the underwater cabaret.

Cradled by the Tide

The tide rocks all, with a gentle push,
While fishy friends form a playful hush.
Seagulls squawk with opinions galore,
As they dip and dive, nudging the shore.

A clam in a costume, quite the sight,
Sings to the breeze with all of its might.
"And what did the coral say to the reef?
Get your friends here, let's have a belief!"

With laughter that bubbles, they all unite,
Creating a carnival, pure delight.
The tide, a cradle, swings them near,
In the joyful shouts, there's plenty of cheer.

So dance with me under the sea,
With echoes of chuckles, laughs, and glee.
A world wrapped in waves, soft and bright,
Where the humor's as endless as the night.

Tales of Driftwood Dreams

A piece of wood, it starts a chat,
With jellyfish wearing a funny hat.
Starfish giggle with a cheeky grin,
As crabs dance to their secret fin.

Where seagulls squawk and seahorses prance,
The clownfish joins in the zany dance.
Shells tap their feet on the sandy floor,
While waves call out 'Come dance some more!'

An octopus juggles, what a sight!
A starry night with sea stars so bright.
Each wave whispers secrets, goes 'whoosh,'
Laughing with whales, all in a swoosh.

Driftwood dreams keep the laughter alive,
As fish gather round for a giggling dive.
With surfboard turtles riding high,
They tell tall tales as the seagulls fly.

Voices of the Endless Horizon

From a shell, a wise old clam declares,
That seagulls wear the silliest gears.
Oysters chuckle while clams just roll,
As the tide brings in tales on a stroll.

The lighthouse beams, a beacon for fun,
While dolphins play tag in the run.
Seashells gossip in a bubbly spree,
Reciting adventures with great glee.

Whales make sounds that tickle the air,
Cackling jokes while we stop and stare.
Rays glide by, with a wink they say,
"You're too serious, come out and play!"

With salt in the air, and laughter that soars,
The horizon echoes with chuckling roars.
For who needs silence when joy's in the bay?
Here, every rippling wave leads to play.

Calling from the Depths

A mermaid sings to the fish with flair,
With bubbles bursting, she flips her hair.
Cranky old lobsters try to resist,
But who can ignore such a bubbly list?

An eel tells jokes about electric dreams,
While clams react with their guffaws and beams.
With coral reefs dressed up in style,
The anemones laugh, 'Stay for a while!'

The treasures shine with a giggling glow,
Where sea urchins revel, putting on a show.
The seashells chime in a playful band,
As starfish twirl on the sand so grand.

In the deep blue, where shadows play,
Laughter bubbles up, chasing gloom away.
Every splash is a story, a playful hit,
With echoes of joy, we just can't quit!

Harmonies of the Silent Depths

In quiet waters, the fish all sing,
Chorusing notes as a jellyfish swings.
Lobsters tap their claws on the beat,
Creating a rhythm that can't be beat.

Barnacles giggle as currents swirl,
While sea cucumbers do a slow twirl.
Turtles hum tunes, making waves cheer,
While sunsets paint the sea crystal clear.

With every wave, a new jest arises,
Bubbles popping like funny surprises.
In the deep, mischief floats with ease,
The denizens chuckle with the softest breeze.

So here's to the depths where laughter hides,
In playful currents and swirling tides.
The calmness brings giggles with every breath,
In the harmonious depths, nothing is left.

Voices of a Thousand Waters

Splashing jokes from the deep blue,
Sea creatures giggle, what a view!
A crab tells tales of sandy woes,
While the fish sing songs as the tide flows.

Seagulls squawk in a chirpy tone,
Making puns that tickle the bone.
A dolphin flips with a gleeful shout,
"Life's a splash, let's jump about!"

Starfish wink with their five-point charm,
"Stay a while, we mean no harm!"
The waves roll in, a comic relief,
With salty laughter beyond belief.

So let's dance in this salty spree,
Join the revelry of the sea!
For beneath the sun's bright glow,
There's always humor in the ebb and flow.

Waves in a Whispering Gaze

Gentle ripples tickle the shore,
Whispers of giggles, wanting more.
A wave rolls up with a playful nudge,
"Hey there, beach bum, don't you judge!"

Tide pools bubble like a pot of stew,
As crabs perform in front of a view.
Seashells gossip with tales so lovely,
"Trust us, love—we're far from grumpy!"

Surfboards glide, then wipeouts rule,
Riding waves like a clumsy fool.
The ocean plays tricks, oh what a tease,
Where laughter dances on salty breeze.

So splash in the fun, let worries flee,
Join the waves' wild jubilee!
Under moonlight, a cheer arises,
With ocean's humor, life surprises.

Echo of the Marine Night

Whales croon songs that echo and swell,
Tales of seaweed and jellyfish dwell.
Octopuses chuckle in colors so bright,
"Who needs a date when you've got this night?"

Pirates of the deep laugh at old sails,
While sea turtles share absurd tales.
The moon glimmers, a spotlight above,
On a dancing scene that's filled with love.

Crabs in tuxedos throw a grand ball,
While fish in bow ties swallow it all.
A conch shell shouts, "Hey, hear my song!"
"In the still of night, we can't go wrong!"

Under starlight, the mishaps flow,
With laughter shared in waves that glow.
So gather 'round this midnight show,
Where humor drips in the ebb and flow.

The Call of the Horizon's Edge

At dawn, the waters giggle and sway,
As sunbeams poke in a playful way.
A clam declares in a voice so spry,
"Here comes the sun, oh my, oh my!"

Pelicans dive for an airborne snack,
"Just watch me land!" They never lack.
The horizon winks with a flirty tease,
"Catch me if you can, just feel the breeze!"

The tide pops up with a silly cheer,
"Why go inland? The fun is here!"
Mermaid giggles drift past the sand,
"Life's a treasure, you just gotta stand!"

So let's explore this vibrant tale,
Each wave has secrets that never pale.
With laughter echoing on the ridge,
Join the fun at the horizon's edge!

Echoing Shores

Waves whisper secrets, so loud yet so shy,
A crab in a tuxedo waves you goodbye.
Seagulls are laughing, they squawk and they dive,
While fish do the cha-cha, fully alive!

Paddling in puddles, a child makes a splash,
A beach ball flies past, with a great, goofy crash.
The treasure maps lead to a bucket of fries,
As seaweed plays tricks, a wig in disguise.

Dolphins flip stories that nobody knows,
Fish argue with clowns over who has the toes.
An octopus juggles, quite proud of his art,
While a starfish replays the role of a heart.

On shores full of giggles, the tide rolls with glee,
Come dance with the foam, be as silly as me!
Every splash tells a joke, every ripple a pun,
In the kingdom of bubbles, laughter's our run!

A Dance of Foam and Light

Bubbles bounce happily, twirling in pairs,
As sandcastles chuckle and flaunt their affairs.
The sun winks at mermaids who flipped their last hair,
While fish form a conga, what a whimsical flair!

An octopus wearing a hat made of shells,
Jokes with the sea urchins, oh how everyone yells!
Crabs trot with rhythm, they've got the right beat,
While snails slip and slide on their own little street.

The tide tickles toes, a giggle escapes,
As seahorses dance in their marvelous capes.
A turtle named Timmy claims he's a great star,
While clowns toss sea cucumbers near and far.

The ocean sparkles brightly, like gems in the sun,
In this frothy circus, oh, we all have such fun!
So let's twirl with the waves in this joyful delight,
With bubblegum dreams, everything feels just right!

Silken Tides

The tides wear their silk like a floaty parade,
While surfers try to master the wave they just made.
A starfish is whispering jokes to a clam,
And dolphins respond with a bubble-filled slam.

The seaweed is dancing, it shimmies and shakes,
While tall tales are woven, with odd little breaks.
A crab juggles pebbles, his own little show,
As tides roll in laughter, a watery flow.

Seagulls squabble over their daily bread slice,
Turtles munch slowly, saying, "Ain't life nice?"
With each wave that crashes, a comedic twist,
Life's an endless giggle, you won't want to miss!

In the shimmer of twilight, silly tales take flight,
As the moon whispers promises to the night.
So let's laugh with the breeze and roll with the foam,
In the dance of the tides, together we roam!

Tales from the Ocean's Heart

In whispers and giggles, the waves weave their song,
Where even the fishies think 'normal' is wrong.
A crab in a scarf does a jig on the sand,
While clams make up stories that drift through the land.

Waves carry tall tales of the sea's silly past,
Where food chains are altered, nothing's ever steadfast.
Seagulls read fortunes from chips that they find,
While mermaids sip smoothies, all fruity and kind.

The tide tries to tickle the seagull's low dive,
And barnacles gossip, "Can you just survive?"
An octopus dreams of the world up above,
In his cozy blue castle, he sends out his love.

At sunset's warm glow, the ocean will confide,
In laughter and splashes, the secrets won't hide.
Let's dive into stories, let the silliness start,
For every wave holds a tale from the heart!

Secrets in the Seafoam

Bubbles giggle, their secrets shared,
Starfish gossip, but no one's scared.
Crabs wear hats, strutting with pride,
Underwater fashion, come take a ride!

Jellyfish dance like they own the scene,
In their clear outfits, they are quite keen.
Seahorses whisper behind a tall rock,
Making fish jokes that tickle the flock.

Oysters play poker, pearls on the line,
The stakes get high when it's time to dine.
Clams get nervous, their shells start to shake,
"Are we in a game or just a fishake?"

So next time you stroll by the shore's embrace,
Remember the laughs in the salty place.
Nature's a jester, it's all in the fun,
Just listen closely—there's joy to be spun!

Songs of the Distant Horizon

Seagulls sing tunes, a melodic cheer,
With squawks and flaps that all can hear.
The waves hum softly, a tune so light,
Making beachgoers tap their feet just right.

Driftwood plays bass, slapping the sand,
While starfish form a lively band.
Crabs do the cha-cha to the rhythm so sweet,
In this concert of laughter, they can't be beat!

The sun dips low, casting golds and blues,
As seaweed sways, showing off its moves.
The tide rolls in, like a dancer's glide,
In this coastal show, the fun won't hide!

So if you're ever down on the shore,
Join the melody, don't be a bore.
The horizon keeps singing through day and night,
Let's sway to its beat, everything's all right!

Beneath the Surface Song

The squid plays tag with an octopus friend,
In a bubbling game that will never end.
They play peekaboo 'neath the coral bright,
While clownfish burst into giggles of delight.

Turtles wear glasses, quite the old sights,
Reading sea maps for upcoming flights.
Pufferfish puff, trying to appear tall,
But it's really the seaweed who's laughing at all!

Anglerfish shine with a light so bold,
Enticing the curious, like stories told.
But little do they know, they're the punchline here,
In the underwater joke, everyone cheers!

So dive down deep, hear the laughter swirl,
In the depths of the blue, let your thoughts unfurl.
For beneath the waves, in giggles and fun,
The playful heart of the sea's never done!

Rhythms of the Briny Abyss

In the briny deep, where the fish swim by,
Octopuses drum, keeping time in the sky.
Sounds of clinking shells, a swirling beat,
The ocean's a party, a whimsical treat!

The plankton twirl like they're at a ball,
Tiny dancers, yet big in the thrall.
Even the rocks play in rhythm and rhyme,
Moving to currents, keeping the time!

Giant squid waltz, with style and grace,
Swirling around in their watery space.
With a flick of a fin, and a swish of a tail,
They laugh and they spin, floating like a sail!

So heed the melody, let your heart sway,
Join in the fun of the briny ballet.
For in every ripple, there's humor to find,
In the rhythm of waves, laughter's entwined!

The Caress of Sea Air

Seagulls squawk like wild jazz bands,
Tugging at my sandwich in sandy hands.
The salty breeze has quite the jest,
It ruffles my hair, I'm a mess, I confess!

Crabs in their shells dance on their feet,
Snapping their claws, they can't handle defeat.
Waves tickle toes, a splash and a squeal,
Can't tell if it's the water or fun I feel!

Flip-flops flying in the salty spray,
Chasing a dog that thinks it's play day.
With giggles and grins, we slosh through the foam,
Every wave whispers, "Welcome back home!"

So let's ride the surf and shout with delight,
Dancing with dolphins, oh what a sight!
In this frothy playground, life's a big game,
And every splash echoes, "Just call me your name!"

Bits of a Mariner's Memory

A parrot squawks, "Polly wants to sail!"
While I ponder if sea-zombies are real or just pale.
Old maps and tales, oh what a hoot,
Did that one-eyed captain really lose his boot?

The compass spins like a whirling dervish,
As fish chase shadows, they seem to nourish.
With seaweed wigs and barnacle hats,
The crew's all laughs, oh how one chats!

Fish nets have stories, at least that's what I hear,
Of mermaid shenanigans and faraway cheer.
Bubbling up tales from the depths of the sea,
Even the jellyfish giggle, can you believe me?

So here I sit, with tales yet unwritten,
Thanking the salty air for all it's given.
With every wave lapping, another laugh grows,
In this world of wonder, anything goes!

Tales Told by the Current

Crabs tell secrets as they scuttle around,
Whispers of treasures just waiting to be found.
The waves roll in with giggles and cheer,
"Join us for a dance, don't be a deer!"

Underwater parties where fish wear their best,
With conch shells blaring a raucous fest.
Even the octopus shows off his flair,
Eight arms wiggling, what a quirky affair!

Currents chat about flotsam and jetsam,
Bragging 'bout stories like they're in a phlegm.
Paddling along, I trip on a shell,
And laugh at the ocean's own cozy hotel.

Each tide brings jokes, they never grow old,
With each rolling wave, more stories unfold.
In this watery world of playful delight,
Let's dance in the foam till the stars are in sight!

Secrets Carried by the Waves

Whispers of dolphins drift through the blue,
"Did you see that old boot? We thought it was new!"
Every crest carries tales of the night,
With laughter that sparkles like the moon's light.

Seashells gossip, "We're trendy and chic!"
Telling of shipwrecks and all that they seek.
With every splash, secrets tumble so free,
From passenger pigeons to what's in my tea.

Barnacles tease with a tickle and tease,
They crown the old rocks like nature's real tease.
Waves in a huddle, they giggle and sway,
Daring the beachgoers to join their fray.

Float on my back, and what do I hear?
The sea's silly songs bring me endless cheer.
In this hilarious world where laughter won't cease,
The waves carry jokes, and all I feel is peace!

Reflections on Liquid Echoes

Waves giggle and roll with a splash,
They tell silly tales in a bubbly thrash.
Seagulls squawk jokes, they can't quite land,
While fish flip and flop, doing a dance so grand.

Shells gather round for the evening chat,
Discussing the crabs and their prancing spats.
Stars ripple above with a twinkling cheer,
As the moon winks bright, causing fish to leer.

Tides of Serene Reflection

The tide piped up with a ticklish song,
While starfish try to dance, but go wrong.
A dolphin zooms past with a laugh that's loud,
Making waves of joy, oh so proud.

Watermelons float as the seaweed sways,
While jellyfish giggle in a jelly-like haze.
The crab wears a hat, quite a sight to see,
He tips it to fish, like a true VIP.

Harmonies of the Deep Blue

Bubbles burst forth with a cheeky grin,
As mermaids chuckle, playing violin.
A whale hums softly, but off-key today,
His underwater serenade leads fish astray.

Octopuses juggle, what a funny scene,
While eels twist and shout, feeling quite keen.
Coral reefs bounce to a rhythm divine,
As the creatures of the sea share a glass of brine.

Beneath the Creak of the Hull

Under the boat, laughter echoes and creaks,
As barnacles gossip and play hide-and-seek.
The sea turtles chuckle with shells full of cheer,
While small fish race by, shouting, "Last one, a deer!"

Crabs have a party, it's quite the affair,
With seaweed confetti strewn everywhere.
They're dancing so hard, losing track of the tide,
And the whole ocean joins in, grinning wide!

Murmurs under Moonlight

The moon grins wide, oh what a sight,
As fish play tag in the silver light.
A crab in a tux, he's strutting so proud,
While starfish giggle under the crowd.

Seashells whisper secrets so shy,
To the jellyfish floating on high.
The seaweed dances, it's quite the ball,
And clams snap shut; won't join at all.

A dolphin pranks, shows off his flips,
While sea cucumbers practice their quips.
The night is young; there's fun all around,
In this aquatic town, laughter's the sound.

So splash and play, embrace the tide,
With sea creatures, let the fun coincide.
Beneath the waves, where joy's in the air,
Life's a comedy show, filled with flair.

Serenade of the Waves

Waves giggle as they roll to shore,
Tickling toes, oh, we want more!
A seagull swoops, with a cheeky call,
"Who left their sandwich? I'll eat it all!"

The barnacles hum a lively tune,
While sea turtles twirl 'neath the moon.
A fish in a bow tie strikes a pose,
Oh, look at him go, such fancy nose!

"Get off my rock!" grunts a grumpy crab,
He's the tightest landlord; he's a nab!
But friends find a way, with laughter to spare,
Even the shells seem to join in the flair.

Tides swell with joy, a funny parade,
As sea creatures dance while the shadows invade.
In this watery gala, each splash brings cheer,
A serenade only sea folk hold dear.

Gentle Currents' Caress

The gentle push of currents so sly,
Carries a message to fish passing by.
"Have you seen a shrimp? He's lost his way!"
Echoes a flounder in playful sway.

Starfish lounge, their five arms spread wide,
While waves tickle them, they just can't hide.
"Oh, did you hear? The tide's up for a game!
Last one to the rocks is totally lame!"

An octopus juggles with shells, oh my!
With eight busy arms, he'll give it a try.
While sea urchins crack jokes from the reef,
Their prickly humor is quite the belief.

So come dip a toe in, just take a chance,
Join in the laughter, and maybe a dance.
The currents may tease, but they always entice,
In this underwater world, fun is the spice.

Echoes of the Salted Breeze

A salty breeze puffs up with pride,
Whispering secrets from the sea's wide side.
"Hey, clam, don't just sit, join the fun,"
As waves play tag, under the sun!

Mermaids giggle, making a splash,
Their hair like waves, in a colorful thrash.
A pirate fish grins, a joke at hand,
"Why don't crabs give to charity? They're shellfish, understand?"

The gulls caw loudly, with cackles of glee,
While a starfish ponders, "What's wrong with me?"
For he's stuck in place, in a thoughtful daze,
Wondering how to join the fun crazed ways.

So listen close to the breezy uproar,
As laughter echoes from every shore.
In this salty world, where whimsy prevails,
Joy is the treasure; it never fails!

www.ingramcontent.com/pod-product-compliance
Lightning Source LLC
Chambersburg PA
CBHW070335120526
44590CB00017B/2898